Sentimental

Standards

SENTIMENTAL STANDARDS

POEMS BY

Lynne McMahon

DAVID R. GODINE

PUBLISHER | BOSTON

This book is for Rod,
with love, always.

First published in 2004 by
David R. Godine, Publisher
Post Office Box 450
Jaffrey, NH 03452

LCCN 2004101432

ISBN 1-56792-257-0

First edition, 2004
Printed in the United States of America

Contents

Contents continued

Sentimental
Standards

Sunlight, darling,

makes a toy of night
whose monstrous wedding
submerges once again
beneath the tarp and all
the warping promises
that lust commenced
and trysting ended
(defended, if at all, by
Freud's displacements
on the sheets), repeat
in casual ghost dispersals
the truth of day: we
are not betrayers, we
are not betrayed.

Birthday Poem

Hot, rained-on, packed-down straw, strewn then abandoned
between the rows of eggplant, tomato plants, onion, and herbs,
catches the evening's last September gnats in pale mats
and renders, for a moment, the fall surrender untenable.
Impossible, too, to make this sign—your birthday month—
the winding vine of grapes at harvest, for who could drink
in this heat, or light the candles and praise the cake?
The half-century it took to make the man you are is far
outstripped by the tipped and tilting present tense in which
you accurately move, correcting the angle of guyed bamboo,
brushing a confusion of wings from the plot, and not,
in the slightest sense, wincing ahead to the unfathomable,
intolerable winter bed, for straw, you said, muffles
the living so they can't hear the dead.

At the House of Chow

Finding ourselves unmoored, delayed (the children
    tucked away at friends' houses
for the next few days), we decide to start things off
    with ceremonial toasts,
sake in little porcelain cups, and American French
    Chinese dim sum at the straight-
faced, straight-named House of Chow. Whatever
    vows we are renewing,
love after crisis the general theme, doesn't quite
    keep us rapt on our own clasped hands—
the couple beside us is so compelling.
    In their sixties, probably,
well dressed, handsome, they sit with novels
    propped against the folded cloth
and read steadily through their bottle of wine
    (which the waiter pours then leaves
then fills again at some invisible command) and never
    look at each other or speak.
Contempt, we think, has led them to this neutral space,
    but why bother, if so estranged,
to arrange an evening out at all?
    Not a word through the busyness
of soup—their books laid temporarily aside, though
    still in reach—each pair
of chopsticks efficiently fishing out the wonton bits.
    Clearly this is quite routine,
the steaming covers lifted off, we see,
    on *fruits de mer en chine,*

the priciest dish, prepared for two, which,
    from our neighboring prospect,
looks likely to improve the mood—
    they'll have to share.
Our own affairs seem to have dropped
    from view. The atmosphere's
a voyeur's suspense (but then domestic drama
    is our job, in a sense, the chief
providence that allows us this night out at
    House of Chow—a royalty
check cashed for the Kir Royale—
    we *should*
be taking notes). Who wrote these
    silent readers, this
pair of dons? We ourselves have gone down
    mostly bloody but never
 mute in our defeats and agree (a toast!)
    never to end up their way—
but wait, something's just about to break:
    a second bowl of tea
is poured, they've turned a page,
    and now,
by some miraculous synchronicity,
    without a look,
they mark their places and exchange books.

Marriage Dissolving in the Upstairs Room

Mites in their cypress kingdom
prepare the feast they're unaware they'll be
for flycatchers and chisel beaks. Squirrels on their brown
on nut brown barber pole
race around and down

as if all rounds were spirals
set to hypnotize the man inside, dissolving
marriage in the upstairs room, while the vacuum cleaner
sucks up and lifts away evidence
of each day's brief decay.

Too brief, the poets say,
though art may be long, to keep the nuptial
song and its attendant sentiment. Sediment, he'd say,
for what grows stale derails
the mind as well as heart,

keeps the whole brain revolving
through the puncture wound to the outer edge
and back again, a carousel of pain.
But that metaphor is mixed,
though fixable,

perhaps, if that were all
that needed fixing, a recasting of the vehicle
to make the tenor clear, but he's wearier than he's ever been
of making that third thing
resemblances become.

Third things break
the ground of being, and though it may be true
the triangle is the stablest geometric form, the Edenic form
was two, at least it was till doubt
made marriage food for thought.

Depression Vacation

1. Hotel

On the famous street where the famous pass by daily,
    and the workers on their way to work,
important keyed I.D.s on cotton bands around their necks—
    new style, like clunky shoes, that say
there are things afoot the two of you could never know,
    tucked up in your once-posh hotel
whose elevator's iron grille's still manned by the uniformed
    poor, the concierge in his cage
near the door still seething behind his professional smile.
    Careful English
is spoken here, and up here, in our room, as well.

2. Restaurant

Too late, the kitchen shut, the maitre d'
    ushers us anyway to the little table
with its bleached cloths and vellum list and insists
    the chef will assemble
something memorable for us, just us, just we two,
    and beneath the breath of honeymoon
we assume a borrowed luster. O sad melon!
    O subtle sauced fish
of our long afternoon, we croon, Sinatrafied.

3. Wake Up

Wake up, it's your depression vacation!
   The Rothko retrospective,
the Frankenthaler . . . the city underground
   carries you cleanly through
the gleaming tunnels to deliver you
   intact to artifacts, culture, politics,
jazz, whatever you choose.
   What chooses you is black
and sits on your chest like a heart attack.

4. Airplane

Who is taking care of who? Whom, should it be,
   when subject/object transfer place?
Your face is everything I know of love
   so when it rose up over me
blankly, lunar caustic, I was lost. It took terror
   to get you back, the plane juddering
as if to pitch apart, my starting wail
   which you at once forestalled
not with kisses or statistics or Xanax or talk
   but with, of all things, *singing*—
nonsensical made-up songs with Irish refrains
   about death by lightning,
death by rain, over the yon fields Molly-O,
   and me so choked
with laughing, I couldn't stand to land.

Danger

A thunderhead boils up overhead
in greenish gray and hovers, waiting for the signal
    cell that says to funnel down or not,
      stop our hearts with battery radio reports
basemented in the dark. The houseguest
    retrieves a jar—there's food

    down here, and beer,
a near-party atmosphere, or would be if you'd abandon
    the retreat your attic study has become.
    In the thrum of rain and light strobing
the glass, you're fast repainting the last coat of red
    on the intricate box you've devised,

    love's violent assizes assessed
and now manifested in *Homage to Apollinaire* you've lettered
    on the sill, or threshold, of the door that opens
      into midnight air, an antique typewriter on the floor
with trellised bamboo laddering up through the keyboard
    to a vacant chair. Where

    love used to sit? Where
the magician's assistant (for this is a chair unsupported
    anywhere) would deflect the gaze of passersby
    while the sleight of hand began?
But this must be the poorest trick, for Marie Laurencin,
    the inspiration for that great, sad poem,

won't come again, won't see
the miniature on Mirabeau he's folded in the box beside the chair.
    No one's there, though milky arms
    braceleted in green extend alarmingly
from the dream this box is, and the cracked baby lies
    propped inside. Love dies

    and Apollinaire, and whatever
form the storm takes matters less to you than finally
    affixing the gold-fretted moth, dried all night
    on the kitchen ledge, and threaded now
to the highest step near the painted stars, which keeps you far
    from me, or our beautiful guest.

Wedding Ring

Common all over Ireland, unknown to me,
    (tell me again the name of this thing?)
it's a claddagh, a sweetheart ring,
    silver hands clasping a rounded heart,
an apple, I mistakenly thought,
    topped by a crown.
I still think of it as my regnant pomme
    because it's French, and wrong,
and invented etymologies pass the time
    those days you're gone.
Irish clichés, like certain songs,
    wring from me
a momentary recognition that trash
    sent bowling down the street
by sudden wind, or showery smoke trees
    whipsawing across the path
their fine debris, means home to me,
    and however long
estranged we've been, or silvered over
    by borrowed themes,
these homely things make meaning of us.
    I feel it just as much as you—
that near-empty diner in Sligo
    where you found the ring
wedged in the cushioned booth,
    rejected, perhaps, or lost,

hidden while the lover nervously rehearsed
    his lines, then abruptly interrupted,
who knows how, and now distraught,
    had no more thought for such
sentiment as this. I never take it off.

Junked Boiler

For weeks it was his depression detour,
    this futuristic box on legs,
two smokestack pipe fittings fixed on top
    and glass cylinder gauge
still kelvinating, still in place, a junked machine
    retrieved from some alleyway,
saved to keep him saying grace

which he managed, just, with spray cans
    and brushes—corroded iron
into colored grids on which, each afternoon,
    he ruined into significance
the previous day's despairs. *One day the sun,*
    among other things, went down
he lettered carefully on the top, then stopped,

painted out Celan as too grievous
    for his own decline, first sign
that he was getting well. The hell of sickness,
    he told me then, is intense
solipsism, the world shrunk to your nub of pain.
    But that was never plain to me,
he always made me laugh. After each spasm,

an absurdity. How can they play the World Cup, he'd say,
      Can't they see I'm in pain? Then back
to the boiler again, to paint the pinwheels
      and chrysanthemum bursts
of Orion's belt in the southern sky, or
      entomology's variously winged
and segmented deities, revised or simplified

or erased altogether, to tether him to the next
      day's work and the next,
a Penelope to his own Odysseus. And when
      at last he did arrive
back at himself, Zoloft-retrieved and capable,
      he was able to see the whole
thing whole and finish it, and give it to me.

We Take Our Children to Ireland

What will they remember best? The barbed wire
still looped around the Belfast airport,
the building-high Ulster murals—
but those were fleeting, car window sights,
more likely the turf fires lit each night,
the cups of tea their father brought
and the buttered soda farls, the sea wall
where they leaped shrieking into the Irish Sea
and emerged, purpling, to applause;
perhaps the green castle at Carrickfergus,
but more likely the candy store
with its alien crisps—vinegar? they ask,
prawn cocktail? Worcestershire leek?
More certainly still the sleekly syllabled
odd new words, gleet and shite,
and grand responses to everyday events:
How was your breakfast? Brilliant.
How's your crust? Gorgeous.
Everything after that was gorgeous,
brilliant. How's your gleeted shite?
And the polite indictment from parents
everywhere, the nicely dressed matrons
pushing prams, brushing away their older kids
with a Fuck off, will ye? which stopped
our children cold. Is the water cold,
they asked Damian, before they dared it.
No, not cold, he said, it's
fooking cold, ye idjits.
And the mundane hyperbole of rebuke—

you little puke, I'll tear your arm off
and beat you with it, I'll row you out to sea
and drop you, I'll bury you in sand
and top you off with rocks—
to which the toddler would contentedly nod
and continue to drill his shovel
into the sill. All this will play on
long past the fisherman's cottage and farmer's
slurry, the tall hedgerows lining the narrow
drive up the coast, the most beautiful
of Irish landscapes indelibly fixed
in the smeared face of two-year-old Jack—
Would you look at that, his father said
to Ben and Zach, shite everywhere, brilliant.
Gorgeous, they replied. And meant it.

At the Batting Cage

Though the once-seen, now unseen, may drop away
    and hitter and spectator sigh,
      complaining that the light distorts
the arc of flight, the blinking electric eye that says
the mechanism upthrusting its miraculous arm
    disarms even the most alert—
      it's meant to hurt your pride—
you nevertheless take the plate and set the dial
at Triple-A. Did he play? the teenaged boy

with batting glove and sponsored gear
    wanted to know, which made my day,
      or night, I should say,
as the batting cage became a holy place, draperies
of wire mesh swooping down in graceful folds
    to net and return each ball you hit,
      no misses out of thirty thrown,
as the banks of sulfur lights came on
and the kid high-fived you and took your place.

Cry Me a River

It's the reverse of birthdays, this laying out
outside the meats and cheese, cruets of oil
standing sentry at the table and each guest
barely able to breathe in the funerary wreaths
of citronella haze. Eleven is too late to eat,

someone says, we're past hunger
(we did the last of the absinthe
as the flame went under)—we wonder what
we're doing here, feigning cheerfulness
when the cake appears, applauding

as the fireflies come out. The bad news is
(this from a scientist in the crowd) they're
evolving out of their syncopated lights;
some predator has evolved a liking for
the jazzy lit Lampyridae. The good news is

we won't be here to see. To not see, rather.
This matters, we think, on our birthday.
This stinks. We should fling ourselves
to the ground. But one of us, already down
on her back in the yard, has begun to sing: *Told me*

love was too plebeian / Told me you were through
with me and— swooping up to the big finish under
the trees in the two A.M. torch-lit shade and we're made
entirely happy that birthdays are sad, the way
jazz makes us nervous but the blues makes us glad.

Out in It

The storm hasn't yet kicked the electrics out
so all the houses are still lit cubes,
broadcasting their superior sense to the rubes
caught out in it, though rubes

should be the least taken in, being rustic,
—"unsophisticated country fellows," Webster's says,
but then, confusingly, traces
the root to the nickname "Reuben" (as in, "Face it,

he's a real Reuben") which I suppose
could be a farmboy moniker but seems
purely Old Testament to me, Jacob's seed,
or, more currently, New York deli,

whose appearance on the prairie has yet
to be made manifest . . . Whatever rubric
it shelters under makes no difference
to the poor sod and leashed, dubious

dog caught out in it, a torrent now,
green sky, rushing gutters, hail,
and she (I admit it. Me.) hightails it,
as we say in Missouri, through the gale

which has providentially blown her umbrella out,
whose metal spike might tempt the hit,
pre-empting—forever—such rustic shtick
as wind and rain and firmament.

Pink Rock

He looked beneath the rock to find
the god that he had hidden there—
that's Oscar Wilde on Wordsworth's Sublime,

an aperçu so finely made
it's hard to read the Prelude now without it.
I wish I'd thought of it

the day the rock arrived in its leather guard
and was winched into place in our back garden.
Eight hundred pounds of pink unpolished granite

flecked with gray, a glacial boulder
from Elephant Quarry in the bootheel pits, slow
traveler from the colder ranks of somewhere,

Ontario, chosen as my husband's surprise
for me, a birthday, mortuary stone.
Pink rock, rocked into balance and secured

by gravity alone, a god's egg
I look at each day,
trying to crack its meaning. It beggars

and restores itself as the day does,
faint rose in the first light, then full rose,
then sicklied over like Keats' moon

when the livid summer storms arise—
perhaps that's it? Change and constancy,
like our long-married love, crises

only the surface patternings of rain,
nothing eroding the interior yet
in incalculable grief or pain.

But some days it's a mute reproach,
incongruous object out of place
beneath the poplar trees. There should be

keening wind and cemetery yews
or, further back, the quarry pit
and its huge machines, the human form

a mica speck ant-like working the giant gears.
To end up here is loss of face.
Where's the sculptor that can take head on

the brain of stone and see in it intelligence?
This negligence
has a dog peeing on it. God's egg indeed.

Voluble mute reproach. Like the graffitied
graveyard we passed last year
in the outer borough, Nuñez I

on all the statuary and urns. At least
that meant a human touch, and who could fault
Nuñez for putting Nuñez first? He won

his memorial and gets to see it every day.
Better day-glo paint than sand and clay
pressed to look like quarried stone,

and this way you can read it from the road.
Maybe that's the thing I'm meant to see,
unliftable memento-mori,

though not a skull exactly, no holes
where eyes should be, or clacking jaw,
this smooth, slightly tapering monolith's

a gift, after all, a birthday gem
broken up from earth by ice and avalanche
and set as in a ring on a Titan's hand.

Bliss

Lovely to have snipped out of you the part
that doesn't work and heal over whole—
so tidy and democratically done, anyone's body
freshly washed and offered up, or down,
tilted, the anaesthetist said, so the bowel
can float back and leave the uterus clear.
Lovely to sink into that any-woman anonymity,
numb at the extremities and dry-mouthed
(a kind of mallet with rubber ball attached
is shoved down the gullet to block any bile
moving up), to be part of a percentage
so grandly successful even the hysterics quiet,
whiling away their pre-hysterectomy time
in calming contemplation of their navels which,
soon to be laparoscopically pierced, re-gears
the naval conceit with each interior periscope's
sighting. No whitened knuckles here.
The I.V.d dreaming has begun
and the womb-weary traveler—pardon this last
Homeric pun—is fetched up on the shores of Ithaka
by her husband's particularizing kiss.

After Bliss

Already, too soon, it has given way,
      the days of convalescent care,
me heaped on pillows, you bearing
      laden trays of fruit
        arranged
in pornographic displays
(a kiwi girl with strawberry tits,
      a banana cock and balls)—

all sexual squalor and bliss
      hallowed now and harbored
for a future day; then the play
      of multi-layered
        construction sites—
      bite-sized pineapples
and pear cubes stuck through with skinny
      apple sticks,

and fixed on top by an ersatz
      campanile's reach
made somehow vertical with peach—
      each city featuring an accompanying
        verse
      which sent me off in spurts
of laughing (half hoping the sutures
      would come loose

and keep me fused to this bed,
        these citrus effusions);
but when at last you brought in
        Dante's rose,
                constellated
with star fruit and wheels
of oranges, I could not speak
        or laugh or tell you

the serious thing that poets say
        when they say the clean horse
of courage, or the sorrows of nations,
        the beautiful approximations
                the rose
        of the world is. "By his fruits
shall ye know him," one Bible verse decrees,
        and that is truth enough,

but what can I possibly offer back,
        who have no skill with sculptor's
tools or kitchen inventions, to track
        love's journey to its source?
                The force
        of all such unsayable things
heaps up in cities in my head. I'm well now.
        Come back to bed.

Sentimental Standards

All day, as if all the adages applied, the watched pot
and stopped clock never moved, the square
        of window glass stayed fraught
with yellow (sunlight to this day can stare
intolerably from its mad-making, inching, unitchable

hours)—until, of course, they did. Simmering night.
And the faulty bell half rung, a wrung squawk
        like a hand clapped across a mouth, tightened
the visceral squeeze of erotic talk
the rational self could not shut up . . . A self set up?

I suppose. But beyond that, out in those trackless
margins torch songs arrow in to, the heart-
        piercing suspicion that This might actually
be It. And in It came. You, to be precise. Art-
fully disguising your surprise, you later explained, that I

wasn't the other girl at the game, whose poker sense
was fine, whose high-strung invitation you assumed
        this was. Ah, love. *The innocent*
are so few, Elizabeth Bowen wrote, *that two of them*
seldom meet. When they do, their victims lie strewn

all round. But our victims (mine)
proved otherwise. Bowen's forecast snake, *like oiled silk,*
        like a length of live water, climbed
the sentimental standards in my brain and willed
itself elsewhere. What we dared after that I think

you have feared ever since—illusion gone, our fate
snakebit. But, my dear, it's been twenty-five years.
         I'm still that mistake
at the door, who knew what she was in for.
And you? Still not certain it's not deceit,

keep faith with my stratagems anyway. And raise
my fingers, one by one, to kiss them on
         their very tips, whose frayed
electric charge is shivering yet—in almost song—
to keep the standard set.

In Love with It, If It Requires No Tending

Adam's curse was work, but his gift for naming, given first,
endured beyond the field's exigencies, or slain and slaying sons,
the history of thirst that worsened diasporas and enclosure acts
and land-grabs of the ruling parties, sorties sent out
to annex neighbors, favors bestowed and sown in earth,
reversing owners and disputing births
till each untilled but worthy plot was parceled out
and border wars were made eternal. Property
is theft, William Godwin said. But Wordsworth disagreed.
A scrap of land confers a dignity on man, not to be had
by any other means. O the greater fleabane, Patrick Kavanagh
exclaimed, that grew at the back of the potato-pit! He knew it
was unremitting toil. But loved the language it employed:
Autumn gentian. Bitterroot. Love-lies-bleeding. Adam's fruit.

A General Introduction to My Garden
FIRST LESSON: *The Fall*

In the *Columbia Tribune* a mere paragraph
that this summer storm took off a roof and
blew a doghouse through a chain-link fence,
the weimaraner inside intact, though skittish
now, it seems, at back porch chimes (the owners
vow to take them down, replace them
with hollow copper bells, whose clapperlessness
appeals to me as well, as the form
of meaning, if not the sound), but not a word
regarding you, my fallen walnut tree,
whose catastrophe included mine:
hit dead center on the vegetable plot, you got
tomatillos and tomato plants and two
cucumbers and half the terraced climbing things,
and covering everything else
with your outflung arms, which broke
the heaviest trunk-weight fall, gave all the other
plants a day-long shade.
Well, one might say, this hardly rates
a poem. Trees fall. Blossoms blacken.
I don't intend a message here, or spiritual
aside. What druidical rites the fireflies
invoke for the light-winged dryads of the trees
are invisible to me, though I've read the lore.
It's more that I was a novice at gardening
and was, perhaps, too precious in my expertise.
Too early proud, I confront the harvest now
in narrower terms. The wood will burn,
the stump remain, and I, for all of my

apostrophizing, will have learned
something by your fall.
Cleverness will not keep the tree upright
or calm the frightened dog.

SECOND LESSON: *Spectral Bodies*

What was it penance for, this burbling
        out of the yard at dawn
billions of newly sprung, flung up cicadas?
And what steered the commentators past
        the obvious theme
(out of Moses' dream came the mandibles of grief
from which no field could e'er recover)
        to natural selection
and their place in the scheme? Billions born

that millions might survive. A six-weeks' fusillade
        in the trees, then the abrupt
cease-fire, the Champs de Mars littered with shells
and iridescent wings. Not a Biblical thing,
        not, at least, on Live At Five,
and all the local gardener could advise
was buying yards of nylon net to wind around
        the tenderest trees.
And so we see all over town these spectral bodies,

gowned in wedding white or prom pastels,
        girlishly nervous,
standing about in flounces not really of their choosing.
Surely this refusing of significance, these defensive
        Christos' wrapping Eden
in secular cloth, must give God pause. As it does me,
whose absinthe-green concoction has become
        somehow draped to take on
a candle's shape, and then, unavoidably, Mary's.

THIRD LESSON: *Drought*

What green clocks the drought unwinds
    in other beds are here reset,
the man-high sticky stems manfully
    propping up the brilliant heads,
seed-studded as if the spill of harvest
    still had months to go.
This Phoebus face, or lion's mane, as some
    have called it, vacantly surveys
the brown terrain it towers over and goads
    the eye to recognize,
amid so much desolation, indifferent splendor.
    What ardor spent
in careful weeding, trundling water buckets,
    reseeding all the other elements
in this hardpan plot, together will not make
    an August salad, and all
the Ali Babas of the gardening guides
    won't describe how best
to eat the flower. Its power seems to lie,
    not in seeds or oil or museum
paintings, but in retraining our ways
    of suffering fools.
The sunflower in the fissured earth rises
    by other rules.

FOURTH LESSON: *Myth*

Like Isabella's pot of basil, but not.
  A perverse, inverted myth
    from someone gifted
with allusive wit, this crock of ivy winds
the threaded ribs of a headless wire doll.

No skull at all, it's a dressmaker's
  dolldress dummy,
    whose adolescent form,
shallow cups for budding breasts, the briefest
flare at hips, suggests that phantom clothes

run up on some foot-treadled machine
  were dreams of teenage
    sex appeal.
The torso's both realer than the steely Barbie,
fifty years away, and more ideal,

for this cage of air, before it rarified
  into ivy art,
    before, even,
the junk box at the antique shop, lived
an attic life—fair attitude!—which Keats

might have construed as greenly suited
  for another poem,
    whose hero's bones
would not decay, whose calcined brain-surround
would not be grounds for terrace gardening.

This might be the other thing, all body,
       no thought—O for a life
          of Sensation!—
bought to please and held dear, whose very frets
and gracing curves still serve as lesson

for all who look: Here is nature, friendship,
       and a love of books.

FIFTH LESSON: *Celebration*

Some great stormfowl has shaken eggs of fire
past the roof to nest on cedar shakes
one house over, wires of smoke drawn back to her
as proof of heaven's woofed attachment
to whatever earthly arsonists would ignite.
Another plosive puff, then cordite stinking
from her underparts, this broody celebration
starts a hencoop of cackling alarums
the enormous cloud-winged promissory bird
—the dove undoved in this mock war—
will not allay. Who plays at Independence Day
employs real sparks. And now the net's gone dark
and bits of plastic lace, "birdies"
they're called, trace an upward arc on gusts
of ash, then drop soft noses in the grass.

SIXTH LESSON: *Erosion*

These rocks, plucked like rusty fruit from the granite field
at the construction site, were never so inviting as today
when, heaped into a rockery, they gave
each hand-sized face to light as if this height of summer,
Solstice Celebration Day, meant to make a pink-lit temple
at the lip of the ravine.
                         It seemed a different thing
to take them down, reground them into useful lines
runneling the creekbed to the wash. To hold erosion
to a human pace, though a necessity,
could not assuage my sense that monuments
heap up, not down, and should stay visible from
the back porch steps. The heft and loft of each rock
                         we heaved to disappear into the snarl
of vines reclimbed the aching musculature to settle
in my head. Rocks mark the place the living
cede the dead, but our garden Buddha, calm
at the head of the rocked-in creek, repeats instead his scholar
protégé Wang Wei: No one can tell which way
                         may flow the stream of paradise.

SEVENTH LESSON: *Absence*

It was exactly as the name implied,
the smoketree's ashy winter skein, a kind
of gray diaphane whose nets could bind
hoarfrost to light

to smoky thaw, until all
resemblance to greening summer died.
It was best then, as a mausoleum thing, beside
the nuded sticks of balding

cypress which fixed it otherwise
in spring, when one took all the coins of sun
and left the other poor. Then
it beggared sideways

to the walk, importuning light,
brushing its fragile would-be ash
against our heads and arms, lashing,
annoying. The plight

of trees without Ovidian myth
is harsh, an inconvenience obscuring steps.
We finally cut it down. Death, I guess,
seems apt, if cryptic,

eternal winter and all that.
And naturally we miss it (our nature to pine
whatever's gone, even if by our own design).
Our son Zach

recently read his third-grade theme
which told of a lady's "fatal death"
and his own disgruntlement at the theft
of what he calls his "self of steam,"

not relevant, perhaps,
to the newly mulched space beside the door,
but that a ghost-self, smoke-self, hovers
over the penciled page—

the paper, too, a dividend
of death, yellow lumber to yellow sheet—
makes me think it is complete,
even if its meaning tends

like family gardening
to keep benign all signs of sorrow.
The lady dies fatally in his arms.
The hero wakes up screaming.

EIGHTH LESSON: *Work*

Eight pick-up loads of red mulch later
he's finally through, save for the crude cairn
of rocks he's excavated at some cost to shovel head
and his slightly more frangible own

(tenderly shaded by a cowboy straw
which he doffs, now and then,
to my smothered mirth—Missy, he drawls,
come put your hands in dirt).

It's all hard work, stoop
and heave through radiant dapples,
the poplar beside him casting its green sieve
of shadows across his back

and neck, not shade enough
to keep his neckerchief dry
(fastened bandana-fashion in a noose)
but, given the illusion

of breeze that moving leaves
creates, enough to make him
grateful. The landscape is beginning to resemble
his intent:

Bushido bonsai, unminiaturized.
The six foot arms of juniper devise
a twisting, outflung, impenetrable maze, prickling
around its crippled center—

some car, we think, took the corner
fast, came crashing into it—
which he extricates with a pruning saw till all
the death-burnt limbs are gone.

What's left is less a Japanese
retreat, though it is that too,
with its stone bench and pagoda lantern, than a pattern
I perceive in all his work,

wholeness lifted out of smash,
past injury consigned to past.
And kindness, which defines him most, and
his not knowing this.

On Deciding to Fire My Chiropractor

The clipped-up x-ray appears to show
     my bones beginning a scoliote sway,
the vertebral swerve toward cervical lock
     (the doctor points
with a sharpened stick) which fixes my head
     beyond my neck.
And that's bad, I guess, for he next begins
     listing bits
from my skeletal past which will no doubt
     accelerate my swift
decline. . . . But I'm less aghast than
     he thinks right; in fact
I'm rather moved by the former lives
     alluded to. Those bone spurs
on the pelvic saddle? A cowgirl grace, some
     hormone-addled gyno-trace
still fording rills across the long-ago. I'm
     fond of those.
That catch and release in the middle back?
     Channels for the schooling
fish whose oiled omega-darting kept
     the mother limber
as she bent. Love's integument.
     Well, then, if not
the past (he snaps the x-ray off the screen)
     what about
the coming strains? The years that bring
     the inevitable stress?

I've read my Horace, I know the drill:
    the middle way,
the cautious life—so I fire him
    and take my mat
to the Yoga Pagoda on Forum Drive.
    No moderate Horace
whose less is more, my force is gathering
    to Catullan excess.
And the problematic once-fused neck?
    Now eeling into tantric sex.

Brit Lit Survey: Blake to Larkin

My arm-long cache of manuscripts, photo-
copied or pencilled out in spider cracks
        still noticeably fouled
    by tearful receptivity,
are tipped behind my reading chair.
I'll leave them there

for I am done with weeping now. No more
shall grief of mine the season wrong.
        No more
    shall wayward grief abuse
the genial hour. What flowers of long
suffering the poets

planted, what green fuse refusing to mourn
while singing mournful, will all be spaded
        back underground.
    Not for me the involuntary
sob, that globular sound. I am done
with weeping now.

Blub on, ye readers of ditties of no tone.
I myself am stone. Death no different
        whined at
    than withstood? Gone for good
the war dead, disease dead, childhood-
blighted

and massacre-fallen, the dark night
of the soul foul curst, worst,
                    there is none?
          I will stand before the class
and read as one

for whom dignity is not a lost domain.
Surprised by Joy? Ring out
                    wild bells
          and let him die? Our long
acquaintance

shallows out in gibes. The heart is
stapled shut. The Professor cut
                    and dried.

At the Monster Truck Races

It is a flaw in happiness, to see beyond our bourne—
It forces us in summer skies to mourn,
It spoils the singing of the nightingale.

Keats was right, of course, but even those
taut lines don't quite reveal a woe
that self-instruction could assuage—

the age of melancholy gave itself over
to fits of gambling, séances, trickeries,
the usual diverting drink and whores

till he had had enough of London bores.
Undone by sorrow and, it's hinted,
v.d.—the tincture of mercury gives

it away—he stayed sober and trained
his medical eye on the progress of the mind
and soul without a mercifully redemptive Christ.

To live in this world is happiness, he said,
though too happy happy in his fevered state
which abated to a calmer place

only after long travail. His veil
of darkness was rent to show
a summer sky. The greatest poverty,

Stevens would later swear, is not
to live in a physical world, and Keats was speaking
to him there, perhaps of this place

and time, the Boone County Fair in mid-July,
in a country Keats might only glean
by repeating (if he knew it) the erotic Donne—

"my America, my new-found land"—
until George and Georgiana's letters came
and could better describe the midwest's claim

to a glory of birds—they'd given their money
to Audubon by then—and entrepreneurial flair
which flickered and died down for George

but not before they had a child
whose children's children's children might be living yet
in the American midwest,

thoroughly acculturated now, though sometimes struck
by an unexpected canopy of trees
opening above them on their evening walk,

a shrilling of frogs and cicadas in the Missouri dusk
or sudden doves which, lifting up,
might lift them up. Or perhaps

not that at all, but a world far more foreign
to the past, this blast of engines
revving for the tractor pull,

the IronMan's iron weight pan
sliding down the track to stack the tonnage
on the rear suspension—but this invention's

no doubt ancient as the wheel,
tests of strength and machine endurance
fascinated even in Plato's day

though not, we suppose, at the decibel level
arrived at here, where the monster trucks
climb up the hill to wild applause

to await the signal for the grand event,
the double jump over four crushed cars,
a duel between Barbarian

and The Undertaker: "I'll bury you"—
which fuses technological might
and the crowd's desire to see monsters fly,

which they both do, briefly, at the top
of the crush, before the jolting rush
to the finish. It was all intensity

and delight, and kept us in our bourne
refusing to mourn in summer skies.
Then over the intermission P.A. system

the saddest country music hook we ever heard,
"You left a lot to be desired,"
and we walked home in Keatsian words.

Street Fair

He's swayed over to count her cranes,
strung on fairy lights around the kiosk,
and declaim woozily that he planes
balsawood for perches and that she ought,

as befits a fashioner of origami,
to take a lesson from him. To string them
in flight suggests an orthodoxy
he himself has fled, as befits the men

of his generation—sixties? hippie?—,
difficult to tell from his grizzled hair
and seamy face, but he could be tripping
even now the way he stares,

and why weren't women part of the thought?
She's patient with him. For fourteen,
she's remarkably composed, has been taught
to engage just enough to avoid a scene

but he won't leave, and keeps the other trade
away. All her hours of work—those beaks,
those impossible wings!—might fade
into nothing in the carious fume of his speech.

Free the spirit, he waves at the birds, vox
populi, Time is not money! And instantly,
from a dollar bill, he folds a Chinese box,
Washington's face creased so cleverly

the dome of his head becomes a Buddha-
belly, and the gray-green of the bill,
despite the falling dusk, a luculent
green. Beautiful, she agrees, opening the till

(Dutch Masters Cigars), May I buy it?
And he, ever mindful of the stage,
bows as one artful Luddite
to another, takes her dollar and strolls away.

Harrah's

Perhaps a croupier
fresh-minted, just out
   of gaming school (all doubt
     dispelled by the felt
expanse below him, camera's tilt
   above) could say

   with some degree of certainty
the epinephrine/adrenaline amount
   sufficient to counter-
     act the house's take.
They make
   one, don't they, take C

   P R? The defibrillators
on the wall—I asked the greeter
   what they were—exceed
     the paramedic
protocols. The quick-
   ness the innovators

   gambled on—portable
heart-shockers!—have indisputably proved
   their claims. One can move
     more sanguine
to the baize, now that the days begin
   —and end—corpuscular.

Sprat Rain Sonnet

On T.V. it looks like any other funnel cloud, midwestern,
Hollywoodian staple, so someone says tornado
and someone else, erroneously, monsoon, but soon
the meteorologist comes on correcting the nomenclature,
a waterspout—no more exotic term?—whose whirling
out of the usual domain, the Americas and nearby isles,
has made its claim for the record book: this vortex,
in the Sea of Japan, has sucked up millions
of tiny sprats to splatter them in Tokyo.
No one's tallied up the consequence—surely
a few citizens came unglued, a reverse Rapture
in the works, perhaps a skidding car or two—but for now
all that's forecast is a wealth of rooftop garden
crops to come: nitrogenized tomatoes, fishes into plums.

Conspiracy Theory

Some local jokester with an education
        must have chopped the street sign
                no one's yet repaired, Nth Circle,
it reads in full, pointing to a pointless hell,
        half-circle cul-de-sac endlessly turning
                around and back. Too easy
to read in the drought-blasted shrubbery
        and blistered gutters neighborhood decline,
                but that the city or mailmen don't mind
the new address so arrests imagination
        that we slow down each time
                to see what new old instructions
there might be to commend to us the narrow way.
        Yesterday the popsicle truck—I'm
                not making this up—jettisoned
in the middle of the street
        a plastic sheet of smoking ice in which,
                if you squinted, you could just make out
two rods, or legs, or haunches coming out.

Summer Ceremonial

The twilight on the canopy
could be construed as bridal hues,
ivory to lavender to colorless night,
exciting the possibility the two of you
might yet be won to
couplehood . . . The panoply,

though, invokes instead
a dread of all things ceremonial. Fuck Love
Let's Dance your collar pin insists,
twisting its pin a bit further in to prove
its point—a pointed move
you Tom Jones to, red dress

black gloves, black hat. The knack
of bracketing off what can't be got's
a kind of art, and every lacquered
liquored kiss unslips the knot
and keeps things hot—
passionate, in point of fact,

attachable to the panoply
that wants to be your fête, or
fate, let's say, whose music
chooses to finally ignore
your pledges to resist amour
on this twilit floor beneath the canopy.

October Walk with Zach

Why the female moon has an old man's face is a question I can't answer
this autumn evening to Zach's satisfaction. Because it's bald,

he says, and only men are bald? Skeletal dancers
answer otherwise, clattering from trees and entry halls

—either sex, or none, or two do hang upon the bough—
it's almost Halloween now, the harvest moon has a hunter in her

and casts her light-struck chemo'd turban to the ground.
Keats would have found, I sometimes think, in each urchin's

lurching by in sheets or pirate gear, another fear, here,
where Death is made of sugar and foil, chocolate mouths

beneath the masks which ask at every house
for trick or treat. Treat, it would be sweet to guess,

would be his birth night's short reprieve. And Death?
Death, he answered, finally, is Life's high meed.

More to the Point

October occupies our wedged light with whirled
        trash and gimpy leaves—
which drives us to our knees for the brute mistake
of looking up. Scratch again, the holy orders say.
        Let chert, shale, the clapped-out
dirt defeat the shovel-wielders and haulers-away

(who would be me, I ought to add, glad to shovel
        and haul, to have the least part
in the longed-for we. Who sees in each chrysanthemum
he planted a mantra for the coming cold:
        as long as their heads hold,
her flower head holds . . .) What was I saying?

In plural voice, I mean. *Our autumn gods of reckoning.*
        But that's more splendid
than this effort is, cutting peonies through the root
in oxymoronic algebra—divide to multiply—
        solving for spring
what muddy bud sticks will be divining.

More to the point: solve for now. How to worry
        a trench deep enough
to line with manure and layer with peat
as if it were the cossetting earth itself
        and not this rock
godding the peeled stick into Apollo again.

Paiōn Apollo, he was called, in his doctor capacity,
    physician to the gods.
Paiōn! the screamed-out rendering, the cultic
cry, "like a God in pain," Keats said,
    from whose name
we get also paean (hymn, yes, and war whoop),

Paiōn discovered the peony and made it his own.
    But the flower has no
known medicinal charms, nor can it heal itself.
You've seen how the big showy blossoms
    drop their petals
in a week, how the glossy leaves develop

spreading spots of brown, how, by October,
    the plant is hideous
in its neglected dress. If you've driven down
our street, you've seen the curb-fronting line
    stagger.
You've seen gaps in the dirt.

Recounting

The whole idea of third grade math is bathwater blanched,
non-particulars swirling in a nonexistent gray, a swale
of fog obscuring the entire lousy day that kept you in
while others stormed or danced their way outside.
Measuring by tide, by clocks, by graphs' conversion feet
(you're steeping now, steam rising from your submerged chest),
the rest of time meant no recess. The question asked was this:
If the clock hands point to two and eight, Carla was late
to work by how many minutes? Your answer: *Leonard.*
And what are we to say to that? To suppose some other
narrative at play that takes mysterious or frail sublunary life
to the be thief of time? Not precise mathematic minutes past,
but human motives unfolded entr'acte, that you may yet
get to the bottom of, if Time is counted out as Love.

He Stoops

He stops by, casually, to mention
in an off-hand way that there may be
thirty or so seniors
dropping by
to have their prom stuff shot—
not anything fancy, Kodak instamatic things—
we're just to bring them
through the living room
and then out back
to the cypress tree for the ensemble pose.
Does he know, we wonder,
the appropriateness
of a cypress setting? Is he testing
our frame of reference—he did classics, myth,
botany, etc.; surely cypress was
the tree of mourning
in both Latin and Greek—
or is he simply tweaking us for superstition
and sentiment, synonyms to him,
whose throes
he likes to throw us in, occasionally,
to flex his art. (Did I mention his eyebrows
arc up in points, that he was
marked from birth
for Sardonicus?)
I'm just this side of pointing out . . . when he emerges
from his room in half-tuxedo
over jeans,
expertly linking his cuffs with pearls

twirling a blossom in the tabbed jacket slot,
and patently not the Benjamin
we thought
we lived with eighteen years.
Irony or not, all this may actually engage
his heart in some place
just beneath his wit.
He stoops
to drop a kiss on my elderly neck,
then directs beautiful strangers
down the steps.

Ambidextrous

Just how did you learn to write
like that—one hand steering,
at 70 MPH, the other scrawling
cryptic bits on the notepad

fixed to the windshield glass?
Can the brain's eyes divide,
one on the road, one on poems,
and not fly into elegy?

Or are those fragments, as I hope,
evidence of traffic jams, soporifics
for the rest of us, testifying muse
for you. . . .Working one-handed

in the mess of snow or blasting light,
and *night* words must be written
blind (the telltale sign's
the missing letters on the verge,

as if the line itself extended out
beyond the dash to vaster spheres,
drawing its conclusion
to the moon, who knows, of course,

how to handle lyric verse: drop
it like coins from a luminous
purse to be spent again)—
the trick is not to end it,

isn't it? To keep a little back
for the next stanza plan, next
errand run. But gone for
rose food you come back with gin,

an occupational hazard, I guess,
possessing logic of a kind
(summer gardens at martini-time?)
and Biblical provenance as well,

the right hand knows not what the left
is doing. That may be true
for altruists (the King James' version's
key intent) but I'm still afraid

to praise the skill with which you
manage your unknowing.
I'd rather bridge the split. Come,
see what I've prepared for you,

this cushioned chair, this reading
lamp. Interior travel's a fine thing,
too. Put down both hands.
I've brought new maps.

I Watch You in the Rocheport Flood

walk the last dry stretch of road,
wheelbarrowing past the National Guard
stacks of burlap like flattened cartoon men
to be plumped into transitory life again
and passed along hand over hand, eddying
trickles of sandy silicate sent to stanch
what will not be stanched or dammed.
I lose you briefly amid bandannaed men
who bend and lift in tandem and think
that this might be the heaven of community
the isolato's dreamed of all his life,
called into being by emergency, temporary
and therefore free of politics, religion, indigenous
beliefs, though some can surely hear the river speak
and interpret for the barriered rest.
The working quiet's what I notice best
until the nurses in their *gros pirogues*
arrive like Cleopatras to such applause
as men can muster in their sodden gloves
and push forward arms for alcohol swabs
and tetanus shots before resuming their defense
on the not-yet-ruined porches in the gathering dusk,
the filthy water above their knees,
the Red Cross moving off downstream.

Fedora

For years, atop the coatrack's knob, it's perched
like a movie star emblem for a leading man
or furtive crook, a chocolate-brown fedora
faintly mackled and stained by inclemencies
chronically catching you unaware (hail once,

and several snows that seemed to blow up
out of cloudless skies one block from home)—
the snap brim's less than snappy now,
the cleft a bit less knife-impressed, nevertheless
a beautiful hat for your beautiful head.

Stupid how glutted with sentiment I allow
some things to hallow an otherwise ordinary space,
but you have such grace sometimes,
to give my father the earlier version of this hat
because his own father had worn one

after the war—then it was months before
you found another. This one always conjures
its twin and, despite whatever Freud would say,
I'm happy your wearing it summons him.
Husband, father, and now both our sons

have tried it on and briefly become
taller, grimmer, a menacing glower
in their sidelong glance and silent moves
through intrigue and criminal romance,
the chance to make a killing score,

or more intriguing still, the foregone,
concluding walk to the electric chair.
They think it's funny you wear it
as a regular hat. They prefer
the ubiquitous baseball cap,

a cherished anonymity
in every outward sign that lets them,
perhaps, invent themselves inside—
a self you've already formed, or found,
beneath this softening, battered, Stetson crown.

T.V. Ears

The latest gadget for the hard-of-hearing,
whose antique phrase still pleases
(our son once claimed to be hard-of-smelling)
    for simply meaning not absolutely
deaf, though *hard* more often steps

    to absolutes: hard evidence,
hard core, hard up (the poor), hard news.
Hard currency is backed by bullion, not credit,
    though gold itself
is soft. How often must the hard facts

    sink in, as if the mind
was not, was just some permeable bog
obliged to take in whatever's offered, though
    what the mind makes
afterwards isn't clear. Character, some theorize,

    or temperament. Sanguine,
dolorous, mercurial, shy—we may be hard-wired
from the start. But when hearing hardens,
    the star predominant
is shy. Which is why my father, Depression

    child of a failing farm—
hard scrabble, hard pan—knew first-hand
how to be the stoic, withdrawn inhabitant
    of silence.
What a day, then, when science devised

T.V. Ears! Now that
culture can be amplified, he can be drawn
out of his shells. The conch that is the world
gives back to him
his thudding self. He hears it hard.

He Takes Me To See the Oldest Tree

in Missouri, a burr oak, the oxidized plaque
faintly states, which so dominates the landscape
            he calls it Wordsworth
(there's even a companion oak across the road,
also gigantic, and nearly equal in girth,
            Coleridgian in its effort to be
                        the other tree or have, at least,

the other tree acknowledge it). The field
is lipped in tansy, planted in soy, only eight miles
            on the old railroad bed
and we're on bikes, a nothing hike in Wordsworth's
day, but I'm out of breath by the time we stop
            and whatever oblation I've brought runs down
                        my throat instead.

He's led me here for vastness' sake
and elegy: "there's a Tree, of many, one,
            A single Field which I
have looked upon . . ." But what's gone from me
is not yet here, only hinted at today—my father's failing
            memory, my mother's anxious heart,
                        and the part of the poem

I most want to keep
is the meanest flower, which he takes for me
            and places in a Krinos jar
to carry home "in the holiness of the heart's
affection," as Keats once said. Not for the dead,
            but for our own bodies
                        in our marriage bed.

Acknowledgments

Grateful acknowledgment is made to the following journals in which these poems appeared:

THE ATLANTIC MONTHLY: *At the Batting Cage*
THE CHARITON REVIEW: *Fedora, October Walk with Zach* | THE GETTYSBURG REVIEW: *Fourth Lesson: Myth, He Takes Me to See the Oldest Tree, Recounting, Wedding Ring* | THE HUDSON REVIEW: *Cry Me a River*
THE IOWA REVIEW: *I Watch You in the Rocheport Flood*
THE KENYON REVIEW: *Depression Vacation, Seventh Lesson: Absence* | THE NATION: *Birthday Poem* | THE NEW ENGLAND REVIEW: *Third Lesson: Drought* | THE PARIS REVIEW: *Pink Rock* | THE QUARTERLY REVIEW: *Summer Ceremonial, Street Fair* | RARITAN: *At the House of Chow* | SLATE: *Bliss, Conspiracy Theory, On Deciding To Fire My Chiropractor, Sixth Lesson: Erosion, Eighth Lesson: Work, Sentimental Standards* | SOUTHEAST REVIEW: *Out in It, T.V. Ears* | THE SOUTHERN REVIEW: *Danger, First Lesson: The Fall, Junked Boiler, Second Lesson: Spectral Bodies, Sunlight, Darling, We Take Our Children to Ireland* | TriQUARTERLY: *After Bliss, At the Monster Truck Races* | THE YALE REVIEW: *Harrah's, Marriage Dissolving in the Upstairs Room* | *We Take Our Children To Ireland* also appeared in the following anthologies: BEST AMERICAN POETRY 2000; PUSHCART PRIZE ANTHOLOGY 2000; THE BOOK OF IRISH-AMERICAN POETRY FROM THE EIGHTEENTH CENTURY TO THE PRESENT.

I wish to thank the following people, to whom these poems are dedicated: *Cry Me a River* to Penelope

Pelizzon; *Fourth Lesson: Myth* to Karen Holmberg; *Second Lesson: Spectral Bodies* to Bob Watts; *Brit Lit Survey* to Heather Maring; *Street Fair* to Liz Cairns, and *Summer Ceremonial* to Averill Curdy.

A Note on the Type

Sentimental Standards has been set in Scala, a type designed by Dutch designer Martin Majoor in the late 1980s for the Vredenberg Music Centre in Utrecht. While working as a graphic designer for the Centre, Majoor was dissatisfied by the paucity of typefaces available for digital typesetting and decided to design a new, complete family of type, which he christened Scala after the Teatro alla Scala in Milan. Although Scala lacks any clear historical precedent, Majoor's model was heavily influenced by humanist typefaces such as Bembo and the typefaces designed in the late 18th century by Pierre Simon Fournier.

Design and composition by Susan H. Sims